The Den of Lost Hours

THE DEN OF LOST HOURS

BY

AARON BRINDLE

'The limits of my language mean
the limits of my world.'
—*Ludwig Wittgenstein*

CRESCENT MOON BOOKS
Sydney

Copyright © 2017 Aaron Brindle

All rights reserved. This book or any portion thereof may not be reproduced or used in any manner whatsoever without the express written permission of the publisher except for the use of brief quotations in a book review.

First print edition 2017

National Library of Australia Cataloguing-in-Publication entry:
Brindle, Aaron, author.
The den of lost hours / written by Aaron Brindle.

ISBN: 9780987626547 (paperback)
Haiku.
Senryu.
Poetry.
Japanese poetry.

Cover illustration by Lucy Fekete

Published in Australia by Crescent Moon Books
www.crescentmoonbooks.com

For Paul–
teacher, editor & friend immemorial.

CONTENTS

English Haiku and Senryū	*1*
Free Verse	*25*
Remembrance	27
Footnote to Remembrance	30
Appreciation	31
Great Army of Night	32
Sky of Distinct Extinction	33
2B-Shaded Tarot Box	34
Mind of Earthly Dreams	35
Tonight, Hungry Jack's	36
Smells Like Teen Angst	37
Fourth Reich Brothers Association	38
Fearless of The Bends	40
Dark, Winding Road Ends	42
An Angel at Rest	43
Memory in Silhouette	44
Lines of Meaning	46
Heavenly Trade	47
O Promise	48
The Scatterbrained	50

PREFACE

After I had written them, it had been over a decade since I last read through many of these pieces. So much has changed since then, but something was still alive within those momentary snapshots of writing—those thoughts and feelings I desired to explore and hoped to share with others.

So many notebooks that (along with my poetry and prose) had notes from wherever I was, whatever I was doing or planning at the time: London bus times, directions, draft letters of apology and love, and my favourite—Scrabble score tabulations from my travels across Europe in 2007, complete with liner notes...

"Paused to vomit on ferry, halfway from England to France" (that game was completed in Rotterdam).

"Bologna, Italy, having just eaten Bolognese."

I was amused looking at some of the scraps of paper upon which a handful of poems were written—student roll books and classroom site maps from a North London school I was teaching at. Physically, I might have been in the classroom, but mentally I was someplace else.

Always that bit distant—always the daydreamer.

In compiling this collection over a decade later, it occurred to me that there really is no prerequisite to being able to write. You don't have to have been a scholar of poetry or prose—and perhaps that is exactly how it should be.

There's no point in being overwhelmed by history, or those who've already carved out their niche in the world (though admittedly I did find inspiration drinking with Bukowski, riding with Kerouac, and looking for Lorca amongst the watermelons with Ginsberg).

You simply need to explore—go feel your way around this thing we call consciousness—and put it all down on whatever is on-hand.

A simple choice: between doing, or not.

I'm glad that I did.

—A.B.
November, 2016

ENGLISH HAIKU AND SENRYŪ

summer caravan
the outside world holds no light
surrounded by void

the freedom to drive
through the ever-thawing spring
moon over shoulder

handmade from cool silk
a ribbon to tie her hair
guardian angel

she is memory
just a spectre of the past
haunting no longer

nothing to impart
a barren winter landscape
devoid of colour

and I laughed at him
naked in the living room
wearing only socks

dogs piss in public
a dunny for all seasons
I can't lick my balls

a penitent man
would tread the hottest desert
but I have no shoes

you disclose your love
like the breaking moonlit wave
leaving me breathless

no news in this house
a caressing summer breeze
to ease my troubles

winter snowflakes fall
as unique and beautiful
as the one I love

all my troubles leave
over soft autumnal winds
to the world's cold ends

distant memories
haunting my footsteps of late
like winter shadow

these bristly black hairs
borne haphazard to my face
greasy in summer

your eyes and your smile
and a carefree summer breeze
I want such moments

many leaves falling
upon water without mark
Zen temperament

all emotions build
like a thundering snowball
or a honey drop

6 a.m. poolside
Allen Ginsberg ends a set
"Keep it up!" he says

I see a Buddha
so happy and fat and bald
the hardest ice melts

the seasons move past
never hinting at an end
to this used vessel

"It's pruning season!"
says the resting grasshopper
but I stand confused

the summer passes
and I am forced into change
for better or worse

just another day
just another shattered dream
in the marching month

the trees are covered
with leaves of the brightest green
shading my contempt

a dancing moonbeam
flints the spark in your keen eyes
O to be in love

wanderers at rest
by the largest orange moon
in summer night's air

bloom cherry blossom
no matter the broken lands
the skies roll onward

winter reminder
spirit is ethereal
like the bonds of friends

one day I will leave
"Was any of it worthwhile?"
having no answer

something is missing
a clown with no shoes or car
or squirting flower

they build great empires
never reaching for the stars
and remain humble

night covers the land
the cicadas sing their song
weeping for lost love

so where is this line
that separates the masses
between right and wrong

no clouds in the sky
there is no cause for alarm
and I am content

the hummingbird sings
with the beating of its wings
in the summer eve

in this long hallway
there are no doors or exits
nothing but the dark

not one day stands out
the winter passes me by
in a sleepless dream

sweet holy Jesus!
why is October so hot?
my arse is sweaty!

shards of autumn light
split through the towering pines
to my darkened path

as winds billow soft
birds are perched atop their loft
the grass gently moves

the garden in bloom
and the lemon tree with fruit
as they always have

immeasurable
the points of light in the night
and the night itself

FREE VERSE

REMEMBRANCE

Of camaraderie borne from a man-made hell, in a water that could blind and a mist that could draw life—such futures could never have been foreseen.

Replaced by time, we ride steeds of steel majestic, our cares as light as the winds that oppose us—possessing mindsets of exercise as leisure.

We revel in discussions, thoughts and dreams, and the mind never wanders from the present into unknown futures—the only reality that exists is now.

Inside a family home as familiar as my own, we sit at our very own Round Table—aware that certain topics are taboo to ears next door, because an electric hum can never fully conceal.

In the witching hour we are handed the world, where music can be discovered and shared, ideas formed and entertained—we can rid the world of tyranny and save the weak.

As drugs envelop the soul, the devil turns a blind eye—there are far greater evils to support this night.

We sit by a creek-bed on an old railroad sleeper and watch the fires of a great city burn—all the while worried that we are too loud.

An open cricket pitch calms but never ceases the paranoia. Are we even louder now—doesn't this field echo?

But the questions ease as wonder cuts in, and under a painted dome of fixed stars we talk—a kindergarten moon over our shoulder, and the freedom to piss where we please.

Entering the bright neon glow of a thousand beams of light we walk pondering, theorising and laffing—postmodern armchair philosophers, carried along by the rolling sea of time.

O how wondrous the ebbs and flows can be.

Hitching a ride upon the coattails of inspiration, we are set upon by Muse—crack open our skulls and fill them with your word-virus, and we will do your bidding: bedevilling it on the world.

Under a virgin cover for automobiles we smoke, aware of our noise—too many people to wake—while a four-legged friend in its second incarnation circles, lapping at water, smacking in delight.

Make sure you hide that butt well, you addict.

We contemplate cataloguing the mistaken wildlife from our visual periphery—theorising their underpinning scientific evolution, and hope that these nights will never end.

As vital as my soul, how remarkable the understanding that time and space are henceforth trivial.

FOOTNOTE TO REMEMBRANCE

The outside world beckons and we answer its call—
    no destination too far, no location too exotic.
Clouds break open with a thunderous charge—
    ghosts slamming upon the windshield,
    gliding across the ground.
We chance upon Hell's very own kitchen
    where a sign reads:
    'COOKED WHILE YOU WAIT'—
    an anomaly of buildings never to be found again.
Perhaps they never existed...
Dark country roads lined with towering gums,
    wombats that turn their backs at our arrival,
    old tunes filling our ears,
    ideas birthed,
    words written.
Another wonderful course of enlightening adventure.

APPRECIATION

Mind swimming with drink, seated on the softest grass
and I think:

    O love and sharing of friendship!

    O sun bathing my back in light and heat!

    O summer breeze carrying upon it conversation!

    O wisps of skin and hinted bosom!

In the distance, her beautiful neck and shrouded eyes
make me think:

    O blues and greens, stones and wood!

    O smooth bodies that tingle and excite to touch!

    O planes overhead and seagulls poised to swoop!

    O pathway of learning so impossible to reach!

Surrounded by beauty,

    as lovers practice French,

    all I do is stare into a blade of grass—

    with so much truth in the world,

    how can I be expected to dream?

GREAT ARMY OF NIGHT

Soft winds from their journey over untouched plains make their way across the divided lands of the country, carrying the history of the ages upon their backs.

In the distance the many cities emit their unnatural glow, a false twilight spreading silent calm all the same, as the cicadas all finish their united symphony.

And some will live to see another day.

Tucked inside their beds, the people softly sleep, with their heads on pillows, their heads floating in dreams, knowing nothing of the world that still breathes.

The night spreads like a great conquering army, knowing that it will suffer defeat in the East, but there is no just cause for retreat.

With that, even the insomniacs give pause.

SKY OF DISTINCT EXTINCTION

High above,
late afternoon,
clouds with flat bottoms
slide across a perspex sky
like dinosaurs on their bellies.

2B-SHADED TAROT BOX

Shaded box readings like tarot,
    where the dark, light, and grain
    read like a manual into the psyche,
        where a pit or a rise could mirror birth or death
        and like a cancer—
            life can be erased
            from the page.

MIND OF EARTHLY DREAMS

Metal trees,
boundless seas,
fire and ice—
a mind of earthly dreams.

TONIGHT, HUNGRY JACK'S

Unhealthy have my meals been of late,
    so too my dreams...
In cold sweat—a yellow snake poises to attack,
    spurred on by its goateed Southerner KKKolonel.
The only retreat—into a dishevelled hut,
    or the fiery fowl of mass consumption.
Heart racing—probably clogged with cholesterol,
    and it's only a matter of time before,
    like a jigsaw puzzle,
    one last molecule of fat damns an artery
    and the body fails.
The gates of Heaven stand before me
    and I read the inscription upon them:
    "100 billion served—so many more to go..."

SMELLS LIKE TEEN ANGST

With the beginning of each day I rise,
> though I no longer know where the nights end.

Surrounded by those I call friends,
> we humour each other, but unspoken—
> we know it's out of necessity and ultimately futile.

I can see the door to the rest of my life open before me,
> but as fast as I run towards it,
> each step only seems to fall
> trembling.

It could not come soon enough.
They tell me that these are the days I'll miss the most,
> but it's impossible to miss that which
> I'm up to my neck in.

So I guess I'll wait and see.

FOURTH REICH BROTHERS ASSOCIATION

A perpetual thought intensifies as I watch them all converse, goof around and rarely work:

"How did I survive this period in my own life?"

I am but a rejection from the machinations of the well-oiled machine—

a survivor who made it out,

not unscathed,

but intact.

And Thank God I'm not religious.

One boy is on crutches—

I can only imagine the judgemental burning gaze

of many a classmate on that unveiling morn...

Deviation?

Individualism in a thinly veiled goose-stepping institute?

It's your funeral, buddy.

Do your work or I'll have you staying in with me.

Staying back.

Doing yard duty.

How about detention?

Expulsion?

There's no choice, you've got to conform.
Just stare out of the window at the black crows,
    bellies bursting,
        on a veritable smorgasbord of mind-rot
        and half-eaten sandwiches.

FEARLESS OF THE BENDS

Underwater—
>I'd held my breath for so long because I could,
>>with an iron lung of infinite capacity and full gauge.

From the bottom of that ocean everything had looked clearer, though I'd squinted through a saltwater-induced blindness.

It was just an easier life to lead,
>one of no pain and no expectations.

Although ships passed in the night
>and though some may've berthed,
>>they'd merely been names painted along bows.

But now I see the sun beading down from the heavens,
>my cold seabed of loneliness warms beneath me,
>and I propel myself away from all fear and doubt.

Bubbling to the surface,
>my iron lung depleted,
>and it is for the first moment in an age
>that I again breathe fresh air—
>knowing though that I chance the taste of saltwater
>from time to time.

But I am not discouraged—
> I am ready.

DARK, WINDING ROAD ENDS

So long without knowing what I wanted—
    it'd seemed like eternal uncertainty.
To've held it once and lost it—
    to wake not knowing whether t'have it again.
So many false starts,
    so many oases on the horizon.
Discouragement,
    crippling fear and doubt.
But now there exists a chance anew.
Now each day I fight and weather the self-doubt.
Feelings remind me of a time I once knew,
    and I'm beginning to know what I want—
    it's merely happiness.

AN ANGEL AT REST

With her head upon a pillow, my love sleeps softly,
    her angelic mask of calm and of peace.
Her body is awash in beauty, and in strength,
    and I dare not move, perchance that she wake.
As we lay, the stars bathe my love in soft light,
    the missing pieces appear and settle in place.
And I appreciate the humbling feeling
    of a moment that makes life worth the living.

MEMORY IN SILHOUETTE

Aboard a dark silhouette we wait,
>occupants in the centre of a three-lane slip,
>halted in reddish hue—
>hunger conquered,
>dovetail exhausted,
>returning home.

The ambience: an MC'd plane of existence,
>where new doors to Appreciation open before us.

Two cars on each side, join us at the lights—
>all flurries of conversation,
>all immersed in their own worlds,
>so similar to each other,
>so strikingly different from us.

On this plane, I ache to write,
>and inspiration births creation—
>but there is no paper, no pen.

I want to look outside again,
> but to take in new information could wreak havoc.

I dare to chance knocking on the door of memory loss,
> and take in the world.

LINES OF MEANING

The lines
I trace
with my feet,
walking to the museum—
more important,
more beautiful,
than the lines I find
there hung upon the walls.
The horizontal belongs to nature,
the vertical belongs to man—
the straight line is godless.

HEAVENLY TRADE

There, in a sleeping still frame:

    a mind at work,

    a watchful gaze,

    a poking tongue,

    a snotty sniffle,

    a bathing body,

    and a beauty that reminds me every day

    that the mistakes I've made,

    the wrong turns I've taken,

    the misjudgments,

    the falls—

    have never been that bad after all.

Look at where I am now.

O PROMISE

O promise
>   whispered to the night,
>   may you endure this dark,
>   this dome of twilight,
>   this forested wall of witness.

O promise
>   collect thine own momentum,
>   breathe, grow, nurture thyself,
>   and do not permit the hunter fox
>   the falling of further prey.

O promise
>   resound like the ringing bell,
>   struck from a tower on high,
>   and resonate as sharp
>   as a needle that pierces the eye.

O promise
>   do not fail,
>   hold by the most tenuous thread,
>   like the beating corpse,

ash-ridden,
but only skin-deep.

THE SCATTERBRAINED

Who drink?
Where make the bread?
What's going on, man?

Man?

Inner space
Inner space
Inner space
Inner space
Inner space
Inner space
Inner space
Inner space
Inner space
Inner space
Inner space
Inner space
Inner space
Inner space

Inner space

Inner space

Inner space

Inner space

Inner space

Inner space

Inner space

Inner space

Inner space

Inner space

Inner space

Inner space

Inner space

Inner space

Inner space

Inner space

Inner space

Inner space

Inner space

Inner space

Inner space

Inner space

Inner space
Inner space
Inner space
Inner space
Inner space
Inner space
Inner space.

ABOUT THE AUTHOR

Aaron Brindle was born on March 13, 1980, in the northern suburbs of Melbourne, Australia. A graduate in psychology and education, he is a published writer of both poetry and prose. Inspired by Japanese poets such as Matsuo Bashō, he began experimenting with English variations of haiku and senryū in the early years of the 21st century. His free verse reflects his influences: the French poet Arthur Rimbaud, as well as American Beat writers such as Jack Kerouac, Allen Ginsberg and Charles Bukowski.

www.ingramcontent.com/pod-product-compliance
Lightning Source LLC
Chambersburg PA
CBHW020703300426
44112CB00007B/493